CW01468235

The Smart Mone

How to Raise Your Credit Score

by Avery Breyer

Copyright 2015 — All Rights Reserved — Avery Breyer

ALL RIGHTS RESERVED. No part of this publication may be reproduced or transmitted in any form whatsoever, electronic, or mechanical, including photocopying, recording, or by any informational storage or retrieval system without express written, dated, and signed permission from the author.

Cover Design by Paul Guilleminot, http://www.paulguilleminotdesign.com/

DISCLAIMER: The information contained in this book, and its complementary downloadable bonuses, is for informational purposes only. Summaries, strategies, tips and tricks are only recommendations by the author based on the author's research and experience, and reading this book does not guarantee that one's results will exactly mirror the author's own results. The author of this book has made all reasonable efforts to provide current and accurate information for the readers of this book. The author will not be held liable for any unintentional errors or omissions that may be found.
The material in this book may include information, products, or services by third parties. Third Party materials comprise of the products and opinions expressed by their owners. As such, the author of this book does not assume responsibility or liability for any Third Party Material or opinions.

The publication of such Third Party materials does not constitute the author's guarantee of any information, instruction, opinion, products or service contained within the Third Party Material. Use of recommended Third Party Material does not guarantee that your results will mirror those of the author. Publication of such Third Party Material is simply a recommendation and expression of the author's own opinion of that material.

Great effort has been exerted to safeguard the accuracy of this writing.

Opinions expressed in this book have been formulated as a result of both personal experience, as well as the experiences of others.

READ THIS FIRST!

Just to say thanks for buying my book, I'd like to give you **a FREE audiobook version of *Smart Money Blueprint: How to Raise Your Credit Score*.**

I think you'll find it handy to have for those times when you need your hands free, but are in the mood to "read".

Look for the sign-up info at the end, in the chapter titled, "***Thanks Again***".

Contents

Introduction

Have you ever worried that your low credit score will cause you to suffer the humiliation of being declined for credit cards, car loans, a mortgage, or even that cute rental apartment you fell in love with?

Even worse, what if you get turned down from your next job application because of it?

And if your credit score isn't in the OMG-I-wish-there-was-a-convenient-hole-in-the-ground-for-me-to-hide-in range, but isn't awesome either, you may get approved for loans when you need them but be stuck paying a punitively high rate of interest. As if you don't have better things to spend your money on, right?

Life doesn't have to be that way.

All it takes to raise your credit score is the right knowledge (which you'll get in this book), combined with time and a bit of patience. And believe me, the patience part is much easier when you know you're finally on the right track!

And what if your credit score is decent, but you want to max it out to get the very best interest rates when you apply for a mortgage or other credit? Then this book will provide you with the tips and tricks you need to get on the right path for that too.

Is This Book Right For You?

Look, if you're already a credit score expert, and you've got a ridiculously high credit score to match, then don't buy this book — you probably know enough already.

And if you aren't willing to put some time and effort into this, if you aren't willing to see it through over the long haul to raise your score, then please don't read another word. I can't provide you with an overnight solution — no reputable person can.

But if, like most people, your main problem (aside from a credit score that isn't as high as you'd like) is that you don't have time to sift through the piles of information out there to find what you need, and you don't have time to sift through all of the misleading and often downright false information to get to the good stuff that will actually help you, then you're in the right place.

This book can be your time-saving roadmap to a higher credit score. It can save you from hours and hours of research, and save you from making credit mistakes.

As long as you're willing to put into practice the strategies I share that apply to your situation *and* take the time to see it through, this book can help you.

In fact, whether you have credit problems now, or are just being proactive and doing your best to avoid credit problems in future, this book can help.

Heck, if you learn even one new trick in this book that raises your score enough to save on interest rates the next time you get a loan or mortgage, the potential savings should easily cover the cost of this book many times over.

At the very least, this book will confirm for you whether or not you're doing the right things, so you won't waste your valuable time and energy worrying about whether or not you're doing it wrong.

What You Will Learn in This Book

I've packed into this book all of the *most* important information that you need in order to raise your credit score. Some of what you'll learn includes:

- The 9 Biggest Benefits Of a Good Credit Score
- The Secrets To Calculating Your Credit Score
- 13 Credit Score Myths Explained
- The Right Way To Check Your Credit Report
- What To Do If You Have No Credit Score
- 12 Things That Might Be Lowering Your Credit Score
- The Best Ways to Maximize Your Credit Score
- How To Find a Reputable Credit Counselor (That Won't Hurt Your Credit Score)

I've experienced firsthand the benefits of a good credit score, and I've seen with my own eyes the trials and tribulations that people go through when they don't have one. Let me help you improve your financial life by teaching you how to raise your credit score the right way.

And believe me, there are plenty of ways to do it wrong — you know, those "it seemed like a good idea at the time" type of things, the worst of which can land you in trouble with the law. (I discuss how people fall prey to this later in the book, and how to avoid it.)

The Benefits of Raising Your Credit Score

A higher credit score can provide you with more options, and who doesn't need more of those, right? Here is a taste of what a higher credit score can provide:

- More options when you need access to credit
- More choice in where you live (because it's easier to get approved by landlords as a tenant, or by your banker for a mortgage)
- Depending on your line of work, a higher credit score may

even provide you with more jobs to choose from in a tough job market
- And you'll have the very best chance of getting approved for credit when you need it

Change Your Credit Score, Change Your Life

All you have to do is a little bit of digging to see all the ways that a low credit score can hurt you. To see the doors that will slam in your face because of it.

"Sorry, your credit score is too low — we feel that you can't be trusted in a management position."

"Sorry, your credit score is too low — we are unable to trust you with a loan at this time."

"Sorry, your credit score is too low — I'm afraid I can't accept you as a tenant for this apartment."

"Sorry, your credit score is too low — we'd have to charge you a punitively high interest rate on your mortgage, and the extra interest you'd be paying means the payments are now too high for you to afford. Your mortgage application is denied."

And on it goes. Slam. Slam. Slam. One opportunity after another, lost, because of that blasted credit score.

So don't allow yourself to stay in that position for a moment longer than necessary. One of my favorite sayings is "Knowledge is Power." The more you know, the more power you have to affect the kind of change in your life that you want and deserve.

I promise you that if you read this book, you'll know a lot more about credit scores than most people ever do — and you'll be able to use that intel to keep your score as high as possible from now on.

A high credit score means you'll worry less about embarrassing declines when applying for credit. You can say goodbye to the days of begging someone to cosign on a loan for you, and hold your head up high when talking with creditors or applying for that job.

There's no sense in waiting. Every day you wait is one more day you might be making major credit mistakes that are lowering your score right this minute. It's one more day that you are missing out on all of the benefits of having a higher credit score, not the least of which is the pride you'll feel when it's yours!

A high credit score is available to pretty much anyone, as long as you're willing to put in the effort.

Do you want the benefits of that high credit score? Then get comfortable and keep reading!

How to Use This Book

I know you may be tempted to skip ahead to the chapter on how to raise your credit score right now. But if you've read my other bestselling book, *How to Stop Living Paycheck to Paycheck*, you know what I'm going to say, right?

Please read this book from cover to cover. Because raising your credit score isn't as simple as just making a change or two and then going back to life as usual.

It's so much more than that.

You need to have the motivation to see it through over the long haul. Because while some things can be fixed overnight, a credit score isn't one of them.

I don't want you to start on this path, then quit too soon, when success was just around the corner — I want to be sure that six months from now, you've still got your eye on the prize, and you're firmly on the path to a higher credit score (or maybe enjoying one already!)

I want you to succeed. I want you to have a good life, free of stresses about your credit score.

So humor me, will you? Read everything in here. You never know what tidbit of information could be that one thing that turns the tide in your favor. What will be the critical pieces of information that help you change your credit score for the better?

Will it be the fact that the new knowledge you learn about all of the benefits of a higher credit score gives you the motivation to see this through and not give up?

Will it be the fact that you'll be too smart to fall for the credit score myths and that you'll know how to avoid the things that might be lowering your credit score?

Will it be the fact that you'll now know what factors are the most heavily weighted in calculating your score, and can use that information to your advantage?

Will it be the fact that you'll now know how to find a trustworthy credit counselor, rather than falling prey to a scammy credit repair company that does more harm than good?

All I can tell you is, the more you know, the better your odds of reaching your goal of a healthy, high, credit score.

Knowledge is power, and don't you ever forget it!

So get set to read it all! Are you ready?

Let's go!

The 9 Biggest Benefits Of a Good Credit Score

If winning isn't everything, why do they keep score?
Vince Lombardi

So you know that having a good credit score is important, or you wouldn't be reading this book, right? But before I get into the nitty gritty details of how to raise your credit score, I want you to have that all-important shot of motivation — you need to be crystal clear on why you're doing this, since that makes it easier to maintain the drive required to follow this through to the end.

And besides that, no matter how much we know, there are usually a few new things we can learn — check your knowledge by going through this list!

Here are the biggest benefits of having a good credit score:

1. You Can Save Money With Lower Interest Rates on Loans and Credit Cards

The better your credit score, the better the rates you'll have access to on many credit cards and loan products. Don't like the posted rate? Your high credit score might be your ticket to successfully negotiating a lower rate!

For example, compare the outcomes of Jennifer and George. Each of them wants to purchase a $370,000 home, with a $70,000 down payment. They each apply for a $300,000 mortgage, to be paid off over 30 years.

The similarities end there though. Jennifer has a credit score of 810 and qualifies for the bank's very best interest rate of 3.5%.

George has had some credit troubles, so his credit score of 620 means the bank is offering him an interest rate of 5% (that's a 42% increase!)

That doesn't sound so bad at first glance, but over 30 years, George will pay an extra $93,000 in interest!

Of course, interest rates aren't likely to stay this low forever.

Say rates go up and a good rate is now considered 8%. Let's run the numbers again. Jennifer gets 8%, and George pays a rate that's about 42% higher, or 11%.

Over the 30-year mortgage, George will now pay an extra $226,000!

So don't be like George.

Here's the good news, though. Even if you're starting out like George, you can change things for the better.

Work on improving your credit score starting now, so when the time comes to renew your mortgage, you'll qualify for a sweet lower rate just like Jennifer does.

2. It Will Be Easier to Get Approved for Credit

The better your score, the more that lenders will beg you for your business. There are big bucks to be made off lending people money, and lenders have found that, on average, people with good credit scores are less likely to miss or stop payments on their loan.

Become one of the "good credit score" people by implementing the tactics I'll show you in this book, and you can enjoy easier credit approvals for years to come!

3. You Will Be Able to Get Higher Credit Limits, Which Can Increase Your Score Even More!

The higher your credit score, the more money (within reason) lenders and credit card companies tend to be willing to lend to you. And the cool thing is, if you leave most of your credit limit unused, your credit score can go up even more than it was to begin with! Current scoring systems reward those who show restraint by not maxing out their lines of credit and credit cards.

4. It's Easier to Get Approved as a Tenant

Landlords are understandably nervous about renting out their property to a perfect stranger. One of the ways they reassure themselves that all will be fine is to select tenants with a history of paying their debts and other obligations on time.

If you have a good credit score, it indicates that you tend to pay your bills on time and sends a signal to potential landlords that you are likely to pay your rent on time too!

5. It's Easier to Get Approved for a Mortgage

Past behavior is often a good indicator of future behavior, and if you have a high credit score, combined with credit reports that indicate that you manage credit well, you banker is much more likely to agree to give you a mortgage for that gorgeous home you want to buy.

6. You Could Save Big On Your Car Insurance Rates

Surprised? So was I. Because what on earth does your credit history have to do with car insurance, right?

Well, it turns out that, on average, people with bad credit cost insurance companies more in claims. So they use credit scores as a shortcut to help them figure out who is less likely to cost them big bucks in claims, and therefore can be offered auto insurance at a lower cost.

7. It Could Be Easier to Get Approved for a Cell Phone Contract

Many, if not most, cell phone companies will insist on running a credit report prior to signing a contract with you. High credit scores are associated with people paying their bills on time, so you guessed it — cell phone companies love to do business with people like that.

8. You Can Save on Security Deposits for Utility Bills

If you have a high credit score, some utility companies offer to waive or reduce the security deposit that is normally charged to new account holders. This is great since if you qualify for such special treatment, rather than having your money tied up in a deposit, you can invest it or use it for other things that are more useful.

9. It Could Increase Your Odds of Landing a Job

Believe it or not, some employers check the credit of potential employees! So this is one more great reason to maximize your credit score!

Particularly if you are applying for a job that involves access to large amounts of money (for example, in banking), or if you are in management, employers may want to know if you manage credit responsibly. Many employers see the degree to which you are responsible with credit as corresponding to the degree to which you'll be responsible with your job.

I cannot trust a man to control others who cannot control himself. Robert E. Lee

Improve Your Score Now, and Benefit for the Rest of Your Life

So I get it — if your score isn't great now, you may feel depressed reading about the benefits of a good credit score. But here's the thing — just because your credit score is low now, doesn't mean it has to stay that way.

With the simple techniques that I'll teach you in this book, you'll learn how to increase your score over time, so that you, too, will benefit from everything I discussed in this chapter.

And if your score is already decent, remember that the more you increase it, the better the benefits that you'll have access to over time. For example, say your credit score is good enough to get a small discount on your next loan — if you increase it, maybe you'll qualify for triple the discount next time.

Before I go on to the nitty gritty of increasing your score, it'll help you to understand exactly how credit scores are calculated, plus learn some of the lingo that is used in the credit scoring industry.

Are you ready? Keep reading then!

Pssst! Did you sign up to get the FREE audiobook version of this book yet? Audiobooks are great to listen to on the go, or when you just need your hands free but still want to "read" your book! Head over to my website and sign up now!

http://averybreyer.com/how-to-raise-your-credit-score-opt-in/

The Secrets to Calculating Your Credit Score

There are no secrets that time does not reveal. Jean
Racine

The exact formula for calculating your credit score may be a secret.
But the good news is that the top credit reporting companies have
shared the most important factors that influence your final number.
And that is all the information you need to get your score into the top
range where lenders are begging for your business.

Who Makes My Score?

There are three major credit reporting companies in the United States:
Equifax, Experian, and TransUnion. Your score at each of these
companies may vary since all of the credit card companies, lenders,
and other companies who have data on your creditworthiness may not
report to all three of them.

In most cases, when people in the United States talk about a credit
score, they mean the FICO score. This scoring method was developed

by the Fair Isaac Corporation, and it takes into account your credit score with each of the three major credit bureaus.

FICO claims to be used in 90% of all lending decisions. This isn't surprising since with FICO, rather than having to look up three separate credit reports on you, lenders can save time by looking at a single number.

You may have heard about the VantageScore too. This is yet another hybrid credit score, which currently uses a score range of 300-850 (older versions had a different score range, so don't let that confuse you).

VantageScore was created in 2006 through a collaboration between Equifax, Experian, and TransUnion, as an alternative to the FICO. VantageScore says that what sets their score apart is the fact that they include consumers who otherwise might not have a credit score at all, such as people who don't have a credit history, or those who use credit infrequently.

Use the 80/20 Principle to Your Advantage

I'm a big fan of the 80/20 principle. Basically, all it means is that 80% of your results will come from 20% of your efforts. So rather than bog you down talking about Equifax, Experian, TransUnion, FICO, and VantageScore separately, I'm going to focus primarily on your FICO score.

Because if you're doing everything right to raise your FICO score, your score with all of the others should go up as well. In fact, I'd be shocked if they didn't.

How Your Credit Score Is Calculated

So, back to FICO.

You may have heard that there is more than one version of the FICO score, and that's true. But the one which ranges from 300-850 is the most commonly used.

And remember, if you are doing everything right, no matter what version of FICO is being used, your actions are highly likely to move your score in the right direction.

FICO is careful to say that the importance of each factor may vary from person to person — for example, someone who has a credit history only one year long will be judged differently than someone who has a history going back 20 years. But for most people, the five main categories of influence are weighted as follows:

Amounts Owed

30% of your credit score is based on the amount of debt you owe. In the case of credit card balances, even if you pay them off in full each month, credit agencies will typically use the amount owed on your last statement as the balance on your card. However, paying it off each month is still a smart move — by paying it off in full each month, you avoid paying high interest rates and ensure that your balance doesn't continue to grow higher and higher.

Payment History

Your payment history is one of the most important factors in your credit score and counts for 35% of it. Lenders want to know if you have a habit of paying your debts on time, after all.

Better three hours too soon than a minute too late.
William Shakespeare

Mind you, in Shakespeare's time, I'm sure payments were made in person so three hours ahead would work just fine. With today's online payments, I recommend you get into the habit of making your payments a few days in advance to be on the safe side and ensure that your payment clears by the due date.

New Credit

10% of your score is based on how much new credit you have. With new credit, you haven't had a chance to prove yourself yet in terms of paying it on time — you're an unknown, leaving lenders wondering, "Will he pay on time?" "Can she handle the burden of these new payments?" et cetera.

This new uncertainty is often reflected by a decrease in your credit score.

But before too long, new credit becomes old credit and any potential hit to your credit score will decrease.

Length of Credit History

15% of your credit score is based on the length of your credit history.

Think of it this way: If you've just met someone new, you probably don't have enough history with them to form an accurate judgement of their character. Sure, you might think they seem like a nice person, but until you know them over the long-term, you can't be sure if your initial impression of them is correct. Lenders and your credit history are kind of like that. The longer your history on your credit file, the more they feel they can trust that information to predict your future behavior.

Types of Credit in Use

10% of your credit score is based on what kinds of credit you tend to use. However, if you have what the industry commonly refers to as a "thin" credit file (i.e., you don't have a lot of information in it), this factor may have more influence than it would for others.

Generally speaking, it's good to have experience with more than one type of credit. Here are the three major categories of credit:

1. Revolving accounts are things like credit cards and lines of credit — your minimum monthly payment varies depending on how much credit you've used.

2. Installment accounts are things like car loans, mortgage loans, and student loans — your monthly payment stays the same for a fixed period of time.

3. Open accounts include things like charge cards (different from a credit card) and utility accounts — whatever amount is due must be paid off in full each month.

The ideal mix of account types will vary from person to person.

But What About Calculating The Other Credit Scores?

If you dig around, you'll notice that Equifax, Experian, TransUnion, and Vantage Score may have slightly different percentage weightings compared to the FICO categories discussed above. However, the tips I give you in this book can help to raise your credit score regardless of who calculates it.

So use that 80/20 principle to your advantage, and don't let yourself get bogged down in small details that are unlikely to make much of a difference to your end result.

Worrying about the specific differences in credit score calculations is only necessary in rare cases (for example, if you need one specific credit bureau score to be high for a particular lender, and against all odds, your score didn't increase enough by sticking to the 80/20 and implementing more general techniques).

What Is a Good Credit Score?

So you already know that the higher your credit score, the better, right?

But how high is high enough? How low is too low?

Let's deal with that now, shall we?

Anything over 750 is considered excellent. You're unlikely to find a lender or credit company who isn't satisfied with a score like that. If your score is in this range, use the tips in this book to help keep it there.

But don't despair if your score isn't at 750 yet. By implementing the strategies in this book, the odds are excellent that you'll be able to increase your credit score to your ideal range, as long as you give it enough time.

700-749 is still considered to be *very* good — it might not be good enough for the super-ultra-deluxe-lowest rates on offer, but you won't get ripped off with punitive rates either.

620-699 is considered just fair.

Anything below 620 is thought of as bad, and you almost definitely won't be offered the very best rates by lenders and credit companies, if you're approved at all.

What Does NOT Affect Your Credit Score

In the United States, by law, your credit score cannot be based in any way on race, color, religion, national origin, sex, marital status, or the receipt of public assistance.

The FICO score does not consider age, salary, employment history, or occupation. Nor does it take into account where you live, the interest rates you pay on your accounts, or child/family support obligations.

Checking your own credit score does not affect it either.

Additionally, any inquiries made by lenders to pre-approve you for credit will not affect your score, as these are considered to be "promotional inquiries."

If your lender wishes to check your credit report in order to review your account with them, it is considered an "administrative inquiry" and will not affect your FICO score either. The same is true for any inquiries categorized as coming from employers.

Last, but not least, FICO does not consider whether or not you are taking part in credit counseling.

Credit Score versus Credit Report: Know the Difference!

These sound similar, but are completely different. If you already know the difference, feel free to skip ahead, but if you're unsure, then read on!

Your Credit Score

Ok, so your credit score is just a number, usually between 300 and 850, and is calculated based on the contents of your credit report. As you know, FICO is the most widely used scoring system in the United States, but Vantage Scores can also be used. In addition, some banks calculate their own version of your credit score for private use behind the scenes.

Your Credit Report

Your credit report does not usually have a number at all, but it does contain all the details that your credit score is based on.

As you know, the three main credit reporting agencies that maintain credit reports on you are Equifax, Experian, and TransUnion. Creditors are not required to report information to all of them, so your credit report may be different at each one. Your credit report typically includes:

- Your credit accounts, the balance owing on each, and your payment history for the previous two years (including whether or not each payment was on time, or late — and if late, whether or not it was 30, 60, or 90 days late)
- A list of everyone who has checked your credit report in the previous two years
- It also shows whether or not there have been any liens, judgements, bankruptcies, or delinquencies in your history
- Your name, address, Social Security number, birthdate and employment information

Who Is Checking Your Credit Report and Score?

Your credit report may be accessed by the following:

- Mortgage lenders
- Auto lenders
- Employers (for example, to decide whether to hire you, give you a promotion, or grant you security clearance)
- Professional licensing bodies (for example, a good credit report may be required to obtain a license to practice your profession)

- Insurers
- Collection agencies
- Landlords

Your credit score may be accessed by these groups:

- Mortgage lenders
- Auto lenders
- Credit card companies
- Collection agencies
- Landlords

Summing Up

You've learned who calculates your score, and the most important factors that they consider (and just as importantly, you now know what does *not* influence your score!). You've also learned what constitutes a good score, the difference between a credit report and credit score, and who might be checking up on you.

But before you take steps to raise your credit score, it's important that you arm yourself with information on some of the most common credit score myths. You don't want to fall prey to them, right?

Here we go then!

13 Credit Score Myths Explained

It is difficult to separate, at times, the myth from the truth. Bob Kane

There are a ton of credit score myths out there, and I don't want you to be fooled. Because in the game of raising your credit score, falling prey to the wrong myth could cost you valuable points on your credit score!

If this is the first time you've ever come across these myths, don't feel bad. Tons of people don't know about these, and the good news is that by the time you get to the end of this chapter, you'll be joining the ranks of financially savvy readers that came before you! And besides, even the most educated readers usually come across at least one item on this list that they weren't aware of.

Alright then... let's get on with dispelling some credit score myths!

1. A Higher Income Will Raise My Credit

Score

In actuality, your income has absolutely zero effect on your credit score. Not everyone has the earning power of Donald Trump, and it's only fair that we are not judged based on how much we earn. What's important to lenders is not what you earn, but how you handle your financial obligations.

2. 'X' Number of Credit Accounts Is Too Many

According to FICO, there is no magic number of credit accounts that is too many. Every person's credit history is different, and consequently, the number of credit accounts that is too many is not set in stone. So don't let anyone tell you different!

Tom is able to maintain his high credit score with seven credit cards, two lines of credit, and five mortgages. But he uses only a small percentage of available credit on his credit cards plus pays them off in full each month. He does not use his lines of credit since they are only for emergencies. And the mortgages are for his investment properties and the payments are always submitted on time.

James has a bunch of credit cards, plus more than one line of credit and mortgages too — but his credit score is low. He has five credit cards that are maxed out (plus he often misses payments), and two lines of credit that are also maxed out. His mortgage payment for his home was 60 days late last time. And at least once a year he's late making the mortgage payment for his cabin in the woods.

In this scenario, Tom has more credit accounts but has a higher score.

Anna has six credit cards that are all maxed out, and she's been late making payments on and off for the past year. She also has a car loan but just barely manages to scrape up enough money to make the payments each month.

Melanie has one credit card, only uses a small percentage of her available balance, and always pays it off on time. She also has a small car loan for which payments are made on time, every time.

In this case, it is Melanie, with the lower number of credit accounts, who has a higher score.

So if you remember nothing else, remember this: The number of accounts you have is less important than what you do with them.

3. Rent is Reported on My Credit Report

The only time your rent could affect your credit report is if you don't pay it and your landlord gets a judgement against you or sends it to a collection agency. That being said, most lenders do take into account mortgage or rent payments when trying to decide if you qualify for their loan product — it's just that this information does not come from your credit report.

4. Cell Phone Payments Are Reported on My Credit Report

It turns out that most cell phone companies don't bother to report to the credit reporting agencies. The exception to this rule is if you don't make the payments and they're sent to a collection agency — that, on the other hand, is very likely to show up on your credit report.

5. My Full Employment History Is on My Credit Report

While your credit report is likely to show the name of your most recent employers, all of the details surrounding your employment will not be there.

6. Closing Old and Inactive Accounts Will Raise My Score

No way! In fact, closing old and inactive accounts might actually lower your score temporarily. I'll explain more about this in a later chapter.

7. Lowering the Credit Limits on My Credit Cards Will Raise My Score

This is another one that gets a big NO WAY! Just as with closing old and inactive accounts, this might actually lower your score. More to come on the reasons why in a later chapter.

8. If I Co-Sign on a Loan, It Won't Show Up on My Credit Report

Even though the loan is technically not yours, because you are the lender's "back-up plan" if the other person named on the loan fails to pay, both the loan and payment history will show up on your credit report as if it *is* your loan. So be careful who you co-sign for since any mistakes they make could lower your credit score.

The only way to stop it from showing up on your credit report is to convince the creditor to remove you as a co-signer — but this is easier said than done, so if you ever co-sign on a loan for someone, assume that you're stuck on there until it's 100% paid off!

9. Paying Off Debt Will Boost My Score by X Amount of Points

Don't get me wrong, paying off debt can definitely improve your credit score. But if you ever read something like "pay off your car loan and your credit score will rise by 50 points," assume this is not accurate. Because credit scores are based on so many factors, it's impossible to predict exactly how much of an impact a single change can make. So don't be fooled by those types of promises!

10. My Score Will Drop If I Check My Own Credit

There are two main kinds of credit inquiries: hard and soft.

Hard inquiries generally do lower your credit score. Hard inquiries include those made by your bank before they approve you for your mortgage, or by a credit card company prior to approving you for one of their cards.

But when you check your own credit score, it's considered a soft inquiry. Soft inquiries don't affect your credit score one bit!

Caution: Keep in mind that checking your own credit score is only a soft inquiry if you order it directly via an approved site such as www.AnnualCreditReport.com, or via one of the credit bureaus and their affiliated sites. Whereas if you ask your banker to check the score for you, then it will likely count as a hard inquiry, and will lower it.

11. When I Get Married, the Credit Reports of My Spouse and Myself Will Merge

If you value your independence, you'll be happy to know that getting married does not mean giving up your individual credit score. You keep yours, and your spouse keeps theirs. One does not affect the other.

However, keep in mind that if you take on joint debts, such as a mortgage, then that mortgage and its payment history will show up on both of your credit reports.

12. Shopping for a Loan Will Lower My Credit Score

Have you ever tried to do the responsible thing by shopping around for the best rate, and worried that you'd be unfairly penalized for doing so due to all those people checking your credit in a short period of time?

Worry no more, my friend!

It turns out that the credit reporting agencies are smart enough to know that this is not a big deal. If all of the inquiries are made in a short amount of time, they will usually appear as only one hard inquiry on your report (sometimes two).

VantageScore even goes so far as to say that they count all inquiries made within a 14 day period as a single inquiry.

So there you go!

13. If I Always Pay My Bills on Time, I'll Have a Perfect Credit Score

It turns out that just paying your bills on time is not enough to guarantee a perfect score. You also have to maintain a desirable mix of credit accounts, have a history of sufficient length, and have an optimal ratio of debt to available credit, among other things.

You're not alone if this bums you out — many people are surprised by this one.

But the good news is that anything over 750 is considered excellent. And whether you have a score of 750, or a perfect 850, you're highly likely to get the same great rates when applying for credit.

Summing Up

Now that you know about the most common credit score myths, you won't worry needlessly or be tricked by them and accidentally lower your score.

But there's more that you need to know before you get on with the business of raising your score.

You've got to learn how to check your credit reports for accuracy — because your score is based on what's in those reports, and any mistakes in there might be lowering your score!

Let's get to it, shall we?

The Right Way to Check Your Credit Report

A good reputation is more valuable than money.
Publilius Syrus

Checking your credit report on a regular basis is important — it not only can help to prevent errors that may cause you to be denied access to new credit, but also can be helpful in uncovering whether or not you've been a victim of identity theft.

And last, but not least, since your credit score is based on the information contained within your credit reports, it's important to make sure that there are no errors on them that could lead to a lowered credit score.

Checking your credit reports can be a chore, but with the right information (which you'll have after reading this chapter), you'll see that getting your hands on your reports and checking them over is fast and easy!

Where to Obtain Your Credit Report

Go to www.AnnualCreditReport.com to get your credit report. This is the only website that is authorized by Federal law to provide you with the free credit report that the law entitles you to.

While you will find many other websites that offer free credit reports, there are often strings attached.

How Often Are You Allowed a Free Copy of Your Credit Report?

By law, you are allowed to access your credit report for free once per year, from each of the big three credit reporting agencies.

You are also entitled to a free copy of your credit report if any of the following occur:

- You are denied credit, insurance, or employment based on your credit report (you must request your free report within 60 days of being notified — your notification should include the name and contact information for the credit reporting agency that was used).
- You are unemployed, but plan on looking for a job within 60 days.
- You're on welfare.
- Your report contains errors due to fraud (for example, identity theft).

Hot Tip: Avoid paying for pricey credit monitoring services by staggering your credit report requests instead. Ask for a report from Equifax in January, Experian in May, and TransUnion in September. For most people, this is a great way of monitoring your credit for free.

Remember: Although you are entitled to a free copy of your credit *report* periodically, you are not entitled to a free copy of your credit *score* — the credit reporting agencies, including FICO, are allowed to charge you for that.

Your 6-Step Credit Check Checklist

Now that you know where to get your credit report, here are the six steps to successfully checking it over.

1. Verify that your name, address, date of birth, and social security number are accurate.

Be on the lookout for name confusion. For example, Mike Smith or Michael Smith is likely ok, but Michael Smith II and Michael Smith I could be totally different people. Ditto for Jr. and Sr. If either of these scenarios apply to you, be sure your credit report shows the correct title.

2. Read over the guide to interpreting a credit report that is provided by the credit bureau.

Credit reports often have codes that make no sense to a first time user. Save yourself the frustration of reading their "foreign language" by reading through the user guide or help files that explain how to interpret the information and codes contained in your report.

I'll admit that it's dull and boring to read through the guide, but it'll be well worth it since it will save you tons of time when reading through your report. And besides, if you check your credit report regularly (and you should!), with time, the information contained in the guide will become committed to memory.

3. Look for any errors in account activity.

According to the US Government Accountability Office, 25% of all credit reports have errors, and about half of those errors are affecting the credit score. When you look over your credit reports, ensure that there isn't any incorrect information, such as claims that you paid late when you didn't.

Pay particular attention to any negative account activity, such as late or missed payments — if the information is accurate, so be it. But if the negative information is *not* correct, you can have it fixed.

4. Look for accounts that do not belong to you.

Make sure all of the accounts listed on your report actually belong to you. Sometimes simple errors in Social Security numbers or misspelled names can lead to someone else's account information showing up on your report.

5. Check for duplicate accounts.

Sometimes if an account is transferred from one company to another, due to a merger, for example, the account ends up on your credit report twice: once under each company name. This can lead to your amount of available credit being reported inaccurately.

6. Look for lines of credit that are inactive.

If you have lines of credit that are no longer needed, it may be worth closing them to "make room" for a new credit application somewhere else. However, I only recommend doing this if you need to since having unused credit can improve your credit score by helping to keep your credit utilization percentage lower.

The 2 Things You Must Do If You Find Errors on Your Credit Report

If you find any errors, here are the two steps that you must take to fix them. The error may be an innocent mistake, or a sign of something more serious such as identity theft — either way, you need to find out, and fix it.

1. In writing, inform the credit reporting agency that is showing an error on their report. Unless they consider your request frivolous, they are generally required to investigate within 30 days. To expedite the process, provide them with all the information (copies, not originals!) they could possibly need from you in order to begin their investigation.

2. In writing, inform the company that provided the inaccurate information to the credit reporting agency that they made an error and you are formally requesting an investigation. Provide them with all relevant information in your possession that proves the accuracy of your claim. Again, send copies, not originals, of any documentation that you provide.

Expert Tip #1: Even if a credit reporting agency allows you to report an issue via telephone, this may not be your best option. Ideally, you ought to have copies of all correspondence so that you can refer to them if things get lost. Make photocopies of all written correspondence, save copies of any e-mails that you send, and take screenshots of any information you provide via online Contact Us forms.

To take a screenshot on a PC, press and hold the Alt button while you press the Print Screen key. The Print Screen key is located near the upper-right corner of your keyboard.

To take a screenshot on a Mac, press Command + Shift + 4 at the same time. Then drag the cursor to capture the portion of the screen that you wish to save a picture of.

Expert Tip #2: When mailing documentation, pay extra for the service that provides you with proof of delivery. This way, you'll be 100% certain that the information was received in a timely manner.

If you win your claim, the company that reported the inaccurate information must inform all three major credit bureaus of the error. In addition to that, the credit reporting agency whose report showed the error must provide you a corrected copy of your credit report for free.

Once the credit reporting agency agrees to correct the error, it could take a few weeks for the change to show up. If you require the correction to occur sooner in order to facilitate your approval for a loan, ask your lender about a rapid rescore. This service isn't available directly to consumers, but to lenders — it often allows for credit scores to be corrected within days.

So say you're applying for a mortgage and correcting an error could lead to an increase in your score and a better interest rate for your mortgage. If you can provide your lender with proof of the error, they may be able to expedite a rapid rescore for you (extra fees may apply).

However, there are no guarantees that you'll be granted a rapid rescore, so the best option is to check over your credit reports a few months in advance and allow lots of time for any errors to be investigated and corrected.

5 Bonus Tips

1. If you are checking your credit report for the purposes of verifying accuracy before obtaining credit, be sure to ask the creditor which report and score system they use so you can check those first. You might as well start with the credit reports that are most important.

2. If you're like most people, checking each of your three credit reports once a year will be plenty to keep on top of things. As for your actual credit score, according to FICO, in a three-month period, 75% of people have a change in their credit score of less than 20 points — in other words, for most people, the month-to-month changes in their credit scores are relatively small. So it's probably not worth paying for

access to your credit score too often, unless you need to know your number to double check what kind of shape you're in.

3. Generally speaking, collection accounts should be removed from your credit report after seven years — if you see any older than that, contact the relevant credit reporting agency and ask if it can be removed.

4. Don't worry if you see a bunch of "Account Management" or "Account Maintenance" inquiries from your credit card company — it is perfectly normal for them to check your credit reports periodically, and these checks will not affect your credit score.

5. To check up on your FICO score, look at the myFICO report — it will even tell you what negative factors might be affecting your score. You can order your score on their website: www.myfico.com

Summing Up

You've now learned how to get your hands on your credit report, how to check it over, and what to do if you find any mistakes. Before you move on to the next chapter, follow the action steps from this chapter (summarized below) to check over your credit report. I'll wait here, and when you're ready, we can head over to the next chapter together.

Action Steps

1. Go to www.AnnualCreditReport.com and get your free credit report. Remember, unless there are extenuating circumstances, it's best to stagger your credit report orders so that you can check one every four months. For example, check Equifax in January, Experian in May, and TransUnion in September. However, if this is your first time checking your credit reports in a long time, it may be worthwhile to check them all at once this one time.

2. Go through the 6-step credit check checklist and verify the accuracy of the information on your credit report.

3. If you find any errors, take action to correct them.

Moving On

The next chapter is full of actionable steps for building a credit score from scratch. Even if you already have a credit score, it's worth a quick read since the ideas presented in that chapter could come in handy to add some diversity to your credit file.

What to Do if You Have NO Credit Score

Optimism is the faith that leads to achievement. Helen Keller

This section is a must-read if you have no credit score to speak of. Not a score of zero (there's no such thing), but just a big fat blank where your credit score is supposed to be.

A mortgage broker once told me that having no credit score is WORSE than having a bad credit score. Can you imagine?

She said it's because at least with a bad score, lenders can make an educated guess on what to expect if they lend you money or offer you credit.

But with no score at all?

For all they know, you could be worse than the worst.

So if this is the pickle you find yourself in, don't worry — with a little bit of patience, it's easy to fix and usually takes only six months.

The Minimum Requirements for a Credit Score

Let's start with FICO and what they require in order to build a credit report on you.

To get a FICO score, you need a credit report with the following:

- Minimum of one account open for six months or longer
- Minimum of one account without disputes that has been reported to this credit bureau within the past six months
- No indication that you are deceased

First, assuming you aren't dead, the odds are extremely high that you can safely ignore the requirement that there be "no indication that you are deceased."

As you know, I'm a big fan of the 80/20 principle. Because let's face it, if you're alive and kicking, the credit bureaus will probably know it. So why waste time checking up on this now, right?

And if by some chance you're unlucky enough to find that they *do* think you're dead, you can cross that bridge when you come to it.

So onwards.

Now you've got to get that "minimum of one account" requirement locked down — so without further ado, let's get to it!

8 Easy Ways to Build a Credit Score When Yours Is Nonexistent

Alright, so you have no credit score and need a credit score to get a credit account, but no one wants to give you credit because you have no credit score.

What's a guy or gal to do?

First, stop worrying. This is easier to do than you might think.

Whether your score disappeared due to lack of credit use, or you're new to the country and that's why you don't have one, it's all good. People like you are successful in getting a credit score all the time, and there's no reason why you can't join them!

Here are some of the best ways to get a credit account that will meet FICO's minimum requirement of one account open for six months or longer with no disputes. (And obviously, it must be an account that reports to one or more of the major credit bureaus.)

1. If They Offer You a Credit Card, Take It!

Do you ever get those annoying credit card applications in the mail? You know, the ones where they say you are pre-approved and all you need to do is fill out the application?

Well, consider them your best friend right now. Verify that the credit card company is legit, make sure they report to one or more of the major credit bureaus, check to make sure you meet the minimum cardholder requirements, make sure there isn't an outrageous annual fee, and if everything checks out, apply for the card!

Once you have it, charge a small amount to the card every month, and pay it off in full when you receive your statements.

Tip: Most of the big banks' credit cards will report to the major credit bureaus, but call their customer service line to make sure!

2. Get a Department Store Credit Card

Often, department store credit cards are easier to get than traditional cards. So if you have no luck with VISA, MasterCard, American Express, and the like, try a department store card instead.

Prior to finalizing your application, remember to call their customer service line to confirm that they report to at least one of the major credit bureaus.

If you can, choose a store that is conveniently located and sells things you need to buy on a regular basis. Remember, you're going to be going there each month so you can use your card and start building a credit history. So you might as well try to make this as easy as possible by choosing a place nearby, rather than something located far away.

3. Get a Secured Credit Card

If options one and two don't work, then try this one.

But first, here is how a secured credit card works.

Whatever your credit limit is on the card is the amount of cash you'll need to deposit as collateral in a secured account at the bank. So if the bank offers you a credit limit of $1000 on your new secured credit card, you'll probably have to deposit $1000 cash into their secure account as collateral. When you cancel the card, or become eligible for a regular, non-secured credit card, you get your deposit back (as long as you've paid off the balance on the secured card.)

Other than the need for a deposit from you as collateral, a secured credit card works exactly the same way that a regular credit card does, monthly statements and all!

Start by contacting the bank or credit union where you keep your local checking or savings account, and ask if they offer a secured credit card.

Find out all the details including the answers to these questions:

- What is the minimum and maximum credit limit?
- What is the amount of the deposit that is required?
- Is there an annual fee for the card?
- Do they automatically approve all who apply, provided they have the required deposit, or is approval subject to a credit check? (Many of these kinds of cards do not require a credit check — those will be the easiest ones for you to get since you have no credit score.)

Remember, the interest rate on the card is irrelevant since you won't be paying it anyhow — you are merely going to be charging a small amount to this card every month, then paying it off in full when you receive your monthly statement.

You can also do a quick Google search for something like "secured credit card bank" or "credit union secured card."

But it's not just banks or credit unions that offer secured credit cards. Even the traditional credit companies offer these products.

For example, Capital One was offering a secured MasterCard with a minimum deposit of $200 to secure the $200 credit limit. They report to all three major credit bureaus and there is no annual fee either. Granted, the interest rate on this card is high, but since you are only using the card to charge small amounts each month that will be paid off in full with each statement, the interest rate is irrelevant.

Do another google search, this time just for things like "secured credit card VISA," "secured credit card MasterCard," et cetera. You may be surprised by the options that turn up.

Another great way to find credit cards that suit your needs is www.CreditCards.com. This website is jam-packed with information on the credit cards available within the United States, and makes it easy to compare your options.

After using a secured credit card responsibly for a year, you should qualify for a regular, unsecured credit card.

4. Become An Authorized User on Someone Else's Credit Card Account (Plus, a Pitfall That You Need to Be Aware Of With This Method!)

Married? Ask your spouse to add you as an authorized user on their credit card — now this credit card account will show up on your credit report too!

(Note to non-US readers: While this works in the US, it does not work in all countries. For example, this strategy does not work in Canada.)

Have someone else in your life who trusts you 100% and would agree to add you? Then go ahead and ask them! You won't have to be on their account forever, just long enough to build up a credit score of your own so you can get credit on your own.

But.

You've got to be careful with this one. If the person who kindly adds you to their credit account has had trouble making payments on it in the past, this will reflect badly on YOUR developing credit score.

So choose your partner for this project wisely — only choose someone who you know has a long-standing habit of paying down their credit card account on time, every time.

Also important is to choose someone who only uses a small percentage of the maximum credit limit, since this is looked upon favorably by the major credit reporting agencies.

Last but not least, as soon as you are able to successfully get an account in your own name, I'd strongly consider getting your name removed from this joint account. You don't have full control over it, and depending on who you are sharing it with, it could be risky to your long-term credit score if they mess up and do something that could harm your score, such as missing payments.

5. Use a Credit Builder Loan

Credit builder loans are offered by several banks and credit unions, as an alternative to using credit cards to build a credit history.

Before signing up for one, make sure they report to at least one of the major credit reporting agencies, since that's the only way your loan will result in you getting the credit score you want!

The way these work is the bank or credit union agrees to lend you money (typically around $500-1000) that you must pay back via regular monthly payments, usually over a period of one to two years.

Now remember, it doesn't take long to get a credit score. You only need an account for a minimum of six months — so in the case of credit builder loans, you might as well choose a shorter loan repayment period to save money on the interest they're going to charge you.

Because once you have that credit score from the credit builder loan, you'll see that it's much easier to qualify for credit cards, and you can use a zero-annual-fee credit card to continue building your credit history.

How To Avoid Credit Builder Loan Rip-Offs

Sadly, the credit builder loan industry has a few sharks in it that are always out there looking to take advantage of easy prey. Don't be the easy prey.

I recently saw an offer from a shark, err, bank… for a credit builder loan that not only required you to put down collateral for the entire loan balance, but charged 240% more in interest compared to a local credit union. Talk about a colossal rip-off! (And, the local credit union required you to provide ZERO collateral, thus making their deal even sweeter!)

Luckily, the sharks are easy to avoid.

Remember, knowledge is power — take 15 minutes and do a quick search on Google to see what kinds of credit builder loans are out there. Get an idea of the rates being charged.

Rate not posted?

Use their contact form to get in touch and find out! Do this even if you plan on using your local bank or credit union — the only way you'll know if you're being treated fairly is by taking the time to see what else is on offer from their competitors.

The main thing I want you to take away from this is that you ought to be looking for a credit builder loan that ideally does not require you to put down collateral *and* that charges you a fair interest rate.

Oh, one more thing. Did you know that you can get a credit builder loan that will pay YOU interest?

This is because the money you borrow is often deposited into an interest-bearing account by the bank or credit union. Sure, the interest they pay you isn't going to completely make up for the interest you pay to them for the loan, but still, it will help to offset *some* of the interest you're paying, so why not?!

Choose carefully and don't let anyone take advantage of you — the last thing you want is to get ripped off.

Is a Credit Builder Loan the Right Choice for You?

The thing I don't like about credit builder loans is that they cost you interest. For this reason, using a zero-annual-fee credit card to build up a credit history and score would be my first choice. But if you have no luck getting one of those, or you can't come up with the required cash to use as collateral, then consider more costly options, such as the credit builder loan.

6. Use a Passbook Loan

These are similar to a credit builder loan. In this case, you take out a loan from the bank, using money in your savings account or money invested in a CD as collateral.

However, many, if not most, passbook loans are not reported to the credit bureaus. So before signing up, check if your financial institution will report this to the major credit bureaus.

8. Get a Co-Signer on a Loan

This option could be useful if you actually need the money you'll be borrowing right now. (Because with a credit builder loan, for example, you don't actually get the money that the bank is "lending" to you; instead, they just deposit it in a secure account that you can't touch until the loan is paid off.)

So say you need to buy a car now, and cannot wait to save up the cash for it — getting a co-signer on that loan could be the perfect solution. You'll get the money you need for that car, and you'll get a credit score at the same time.

However, keep in mind that getting a co-signed loan can impact more than just your credit score and should be used with extreme caution.

For some people, getting a co-signer is a great idea; for others, it's not.

Sam had his loan denied because he's a new college grad with a thin credit file, but otherwise great credit. He has a steady job that pays great, the job market is booming in his industry, and he's 100% certain that he can afford to make the payments over the long term. For Sam, getting a co-signer on his loan is likely to work out just great.

Kayla had her loan application denied because the lender didn't think her income could support the payments. Kayla would be wise to forego the loan altogether, even if someone is kind enough to co-sign for her. If she defaults on the payments and her co-signer is forced to take over, it could destroy her relationship with that person, not to mention the credit of her cosigner if payments end up being late or missed.

If your situation mirrors Sam's, getting a co-signer on a loan could be a perfect solution to building up your credit file. But if money is tight, like with Kayla's situation, consider skipping a loan that will only make things harder for you, and instead, look for a solution that better fits your budget.

The Final Requirement: No Disputes

Last, but not least, no matter which of the above eight options you use to build your credit score from scratch, be sure to always make your payments on time. Remember, FICO also requires that your account have no disputes. If you're always making your payments on time, there won't be anything for anyone to dispute and you'll be all set!

Summing Up

Don't stress too much over which one of the above options you ought to use first. My advice is to start with trying to get your hands on a credit card, and if you are not successful, then work your way through the remaining options. You only need to successfully obtain one of the above options in order to get a credit score, and pretty much anyone can pull that off.

Also, remember to open any new accounts gradually since if you open a whole bunch of new credit accounts at once, it can have a negative affect on your credit score. Better to go slow. Unless you have a compelling reason not to, I recommend that you start with opening one of the account types discussed in this chapter, see how your credit score turns out, then move on from there.

The good news is, if you play your cards right (and you will, after reading this chapter!), you can look forward to having your very own shiny new credit score in as little as six months!

Action Steps

1. Go through the options for obtaining credit and decide which one you want to try first, second, third, et cetera.

2. Research the options available to you for your choice. In the case of credit cards, be sure to find out if they will charge you an annual fee or not, and remember that the amount of interest they charge doesn't matter since you'll be paying off your account in full each month anyhow. For the various loans options, follow the steps in each section to figure out which loan product, if any, is suitable for your situation.

Moving On

Once you have your credit score, you need to know about the most common factors that might be lowering it, so you can take actions to correct it. The next chapter will get you off to a great start. And even if you don't have a credit score yet, read the next chapter anyways — it will ensure that you don't make any critical mistakes when building your new score.

12 Things That Might Be Lowering Your Credit Score (and How to Avoid Them)

It takes many good deeds to build a reputation, and only one bad one to lose it. Benjamin Franklin

Now I totally get that you might not want to think of the things that are lowering your credit score. It's depressing, right?

But remember this — a bad reputation with credit can be overcome, with the right knowledge. Knowledge is power, after all, and once you know what the possible causes of your credit score troubles are, you'll have a fighting chance to take control and fix them.

So let's get on with it, shall we?

Here are some of the most common offenders, and how to avoid the pitfalls that come along with them!

1. Co-Signing on a Loan

So your best friend, your adult child, your relative — one of them comes to you and asks you to co-sign on their loan. Should you do it?

The main thing you need to know is that anything that goes wrong with the account will affect your credit report. The debt will show up on your credit report as if it's yours. Only sign on as a co-signer if you can afford to make the payments 100% on your own if the person you are co-signing for stops making payments for any reason. Hopefully it doesn't come to that, but if it does, you need to be sure you could protect your credit by making the payments yourself if necessary.

2. Opening Too Many New Accounts

If you open too many new accounts in a short period, your credit score could take a downward turn. No one can say for certain how much of a downturn it will take — this varies a lot depending on your individual credit history.

The good news is, for most people, their score should bounce back from this in about three months.

Tip: This factor will affect your score more if you have a thin file. Also, if you already have a very high score, you won't need to worry about this factor as much since even if your score is lowered a bit, your score will likely still be considered high.

3. Too Many Credit Inquiries at Once

If you need your credit score to stay as high as possible in the near future, don't cause too many credit checks to be run on you in a short period of time.

Every time you apply for new credit, the credit check that results can cause a dip in your credit score.

But keep in mind that although the fact that your credit was checked can stay on your report for as long as two years, the decrease in your credit score that results is highly unlikely to last that long — usually it rebounds within a few months.

It's also possible that your score could further decrease because new credit will lower the average age of your credit accounts — but this will have more of an impact if you have a thin credit file. And if you already have a good credit score, the impact is highly unlikely to cause you any problems. So don't stress about it, ok?

Have you come across the hysteria in some circles about how simply applying for a new credit card could lower your credit score? Well, get this: For the vast majority of people, the impact on their credit score will be insignificant. For example, VantageScore only uses credit inquiries to determine 5% of your score's value — they are one of the least important factors in determining your score.

Here's the thing.

Odds are, the credit card company will only pull your score from one of the three major credit bureaus — so your score will only dip at one of them.

So to sum all this up, if you will be applying for something really important soon, like a mortgage, and you need your score to be at the maximum possible level for you, then hold off on applying for new credit until after your mortgage is approved and finalized.

And say your score is borderline, and you might need to apply for credit of some sort in the next few months. If that's the case, take into account the fact that your score might dip into any decision as to whether or not applying for new credit now is a good idea.

On the other hand, if your score is already quite high, then you may not need to worry about this factor at all.

4. Closing Old Accounts

Unused credit will not lower your credit score, but closing that old account might!

Since part of your credit score (15% of FICO, for example) is determined by the average age of your accounts, closing an old credit account could lower your score. The good news is that, often, a credit score can recover from this in as little as three months.

Another reason why closing old accounts can lower your score is that it could increase the percentage of available credit that you are using.

For example, Anna has five credit cards, each with a maximum credit limit of $2000, and on average, she charges about $1000 per month in total to her credit cards. She pays off the balance in full when she receives her monthly statement. In this scenario, she has a total of $10,000 in available credit, and is using 10% of it each month (1000 divided by 10000, multiplied by 100).

Then Anna cancels four of those credit cards because she doesn't use them very much. She continues to charge $1000 per month to her remaining credit card, but now her total available credit is only $2000. This means she is now using 50% of her available credit. Her credit score drops.

Tips for Credit Card Accounts

If your credit card has an annual fee that is causing you to cancel the account, call the credit card company and see if they will waive the fee in exchange for keeping you as a customer, or give you a different card with the same limit that doesn't have a fee.

If you must close an account, call up another one of your credit card companies and get them to raise the limit on your other card so your total available access to credit remains the same.

Tip: This factor will affect your score more if you have a thin file. Also, if you already have a very high score, you won't need to worry about this factor as much since even if your score is lowered a bit, your score will likely still be considered high.

5. Increasing Your Balance Owing on Your Credit Card

Increasing a credit card balance can lower your score. And it's worse if the balance is high for a prolonged period.

The effects vary depending on your credit file, but here are a few examples of how your score could be affected.

If you have a very high credit score, and you max out a credit card, it could decrease your credit score by 90-110 points. If you have a lower score and do this, they say your score could drop by 55-75 points. However, if you knock your balance down to 30% or less of the allowable limit, your score could bounce back to its original value within as little as two or three months.

6. Missing a Payment

Ok, so it's pretty much inevitable that at some point in your life, you're going to miss a payment. Sure, maybe not on purpose, but sometimes life just gets in the way and we forget, right?

But try to keep those oversights to an absolute minimum because, depending on the circumstances, a missed payment could lead to a big decrease in your credit score.

If you miss a payment and have a high credit score, your score could drop by as much as 70-100 points. If you have a lower credit score to begin with, your score shouldn't drop by quite as much, although it could still take a substantial hit.

The later you are in making up the missed payment, the worse the effects on your score.

A rule of thumb is that the effects of a missed payment on your credit score will go away after two years.

7. Bad Debts

If you're ever in the unfortunate position to be fighting over a contested account with a creditor, it's often in your best interest to pay it now and fight for a refund later.

Now, by all means, put off paying for a while if you know you have time to fight it before they send it to collections or report a missed payment directly to the credit bureaus. All I'm saying is if they're threatening to send it to collections or report it right now, you ought to strongly consider just paying it.

Because if you don't pay it, and it ends up being sent to a collections agency or reported as a missed payment to the credit bureaus, this will be a black mark on your credit report that could remain for as long as seven years.

So I'm sure you already knew that having one of your debts sent to collections is bad for your credit. But did you know just HOW bad it is?

First, if someone sends a debt that you owe to a collection agency, it can damage your credit report for as long as seven years, even after you pay it off. That's crazy long, is all I can say!

And just wait until you hear this next story. Things can get even crazier!

Mike had a dispute with a furniture store over the amount he owed to them. They sent it to collections, but he couldn't afford to pay them since he lost his job. He was intimidated by the tone of the letters and phone calls he was getting, so he ignored them. And then he forgot about it after he moved and the letters from the collection agency stopped showing up for a while.

After seven years, he was delighted to see that that old debt finally stopped showing up on his credit report.

Well, get this. He just moved into a new home, started a new, better-paying job, and he gets a phone call from the collection agency over that old debt. He figures he'll make good on the debt; he can afford it now, after all, so why not?! Turns out that after doing that, the old bad debt shows up on his credit report again! Why? Because it shows up for seven years after the date of the last activity on the account.

So, the moral of this story is, if you have a bad debt that you know in your heart of hearts you ought to pay, then take care of it sooner rather than later. Contact whoever it is that you owe money to and arrange a payment plan. Or see if you can get a loan from your bank to cover the debt repayment.

Try your best. I know things don't always work out as well as we'd like, but making a few phone calls to find out what options are available to you now could save you from a nasty surprise a few years down the line.

Bankruptcy

Bankruptcies show up on your credit report for a very long time.

Chapter 7, 11, and 12 bankruptcies can show up for as long as 10 years, and chapter 13 bankruptcies usually remain on your credit report for seven years after they've been paid off, or 10 years if you failed to complete it.

Chapter 7 and 13 bankruptcies have a similar effect on lowering your FICO score because research shows that, on average, people who file for these kinds of bankruptcies have equal creditworthiness

Tax Liens

Even after you've paid them off, tax liens can remain on your credit report for seven to ten years, depending on what state you live in.

Unpaid tax liens will remain on your credit report indefinitely in many jurisdictions.

Lawsuits and Judgements

A judgement is the official decision of a court in regards to a lawsuit. If a court decides that you owe someone money, this judgement against you can remain on your credit report for seven years once filed.

Foreclosures and Short Sales

Foreclosures and short sales are both considered serious delinquencies and will damage your FICO score.

Repossession

As tempting as it might be to have your payment troubles end by simply allowing the lender to take back whatever the item is that you are making payments on, resist! A repossession could end up showing up on your credit report as a bad debt (even though the repossession settled it), and lead to a lower credit score.

Unpaid Child Support

Child support payments that aren't paid can remain as bad debts on your credit report indefinitely, or until you clear them up.

Random Troubles You Should Look Out For

Even simple things like a parking ticket you forgot to pay could end up with a collections agency and appear on your credit report for seven years after you settle the debt.

When you move, be sure to pay off all utility accounts in full (cable, internet, telephone, electricity, et cetera), since they could also be sent to collections if you forget and, you guessed it, that will be a black mark on your credit report.

If someone garnishes your wages (also known as a wage attachment), this can also damage your credit score. Do everything possible to avoid having your wages garnished for any reason.

Here are some of the more common reasons why people have their wages garnished, some of which don't even require a court order:

- Child support payments
- Alimony payments
- Student loan payments
- Unpaid taxes
- Unpaid consumer debt, such as from credit cards

Keep in mind that wages are not usually automatically garnished for those kinds of debts — garnishment is typically used as a last-ditch effort to get money owed.

So as long as you pay your debts on time, whether support payments or taxes, odds are high that you'll never experience having your wages garnished.

8. Timing Is Everything

Don't apply for any new loans or credit cards if you need your credit score to remain at its maximum possible score for the near future.

For example, if you'll be applying for a mortgage next month, I wouldn't recommend that you apply for three new credit cards for their amazing sign-on bonuses. Typically, whenever you apply for new debt, whether a loan or a credit card, your credit score will take a temporary dip due to the credit check that will be run on you.

If your credit score dips too low, you may end up getting penalized by a higher interest rate on that mortgage you want, or worse, being denied altogether!

A rule of thumb is to avoid applying for any unnecessary new credit in the six to twelve months leading up to your mortgage application.

Everyone's situation is different though, so if in doubt, check with a reputable credit counsellor, or even the loans officer at your bank.

9. Finance Company Loans

Finance company loans can affect your credit report differently than the loan that your local bank or credit union gives you. This is largely because finance company loans are often targeted at consumers with poor credit — so on average, consumers who use them tend to be considered a higher lending risk.

So guess what the credit scoring agencies do with this info?

They may associate users of finance company loans with those who are a higher credit risk. As a result, if you use a finance company for your next loan, you may be causing your credit score to decrease.

I recommend that you avoid these types of lenders if at all possible, and instead, stick with your local bank or credit union for your next loan.

Be wary of the following types of loans — they may be finance company loans which could lower your score:

- Furniture store payment plans
- Electronics store payment plans
- Loans from companies that specialize in lending to people with bad credit
- Some car loans

Whenever the lender for any of the above is not a proper bank or credit union, there is a chance it is a finance company loan. Be on guard! The more of those types of loans you have on your credit report, the more likely they are to have a negative impact on your score. The most simple solution is to avoid these kinds of loans altogether.

10. Transferring Credit Card Balances Too Often

While it's generally considered harmless to transfer a credit card balance to another card to take advantage of a lower rate once, doing it repeatedly will look bad on your credit report. So by all means take advantage of that lower interest rate, but choose wisely so you only have to do it once.

11. Incomplete Files

Usually the credit agencies are pretty good at figuring out who you are, despite the fact that your name may have changed due to marriage or divorce, or that you may sometimes use your middle initials and other times not.

But if you're unlucky, they may make a mistake and fragment your file — for example, putting everything under your maiden name in one file, and everything in your married name under another. Or putting everything under your old address in one file, and everything since you moved to different state in a brand new file.

Depending on your circumstances, this could thin out your file so much that you end up with a lower score than you would have if everything was in a single file, as it's supposed to be.

So if you check your credit report and find more than one file for yourself, contact the affected agency immediately to start the process of fixing this.

12. Fraud and Identity Theft

If you've been the victim of identity theft, the perpetrator may have trashed your credit score in the process. Take steps immediately to put a stop to it, and protect your accounts:

- Contact all three of the major credit bureaus to inform them of the fraud (Equifax, Experian, and TransUnion).
- Ask one of the major credit bureaus to put a fraud alert on your account (this alert will then be automatically put on your account at all three bureaus).
- Contact the police and ask them to file a police report.
- Contact the Federal Trade Commission's identity theft hotline at 877-438-4338 to report the fraud.
- Check your credit report at all three major credit bureaus.
- Freeze fraudulent accounts.
- Consider filing an Active Duty Alert — this will stop pre-approved credit offers for two years, thus making it harder for an identity thief to get credit in your name.

- Keep meticulous records of all communication on this matter.

If you are the victim of identity theft, I highly recommend you check out the Federal Trade Commission's website on the topic here: https://www.identitytheft.gov/. I've provided you with a quick summary of what to do, but this website will take you by the hand and lead you through all of the required steps in more detail.

Summing Up

The good news is, now that you've armed yourself with intel on credit score pitfalls to avoid, you've increased your chances of achieving, and keeping, a high score!

Perseverance, secret of all triumphs. Victor Hugo

Action Steps

1. Take note of any items on this list that may be affecting your score. Fix the ones that you can right now.

2. For those items that you can't fix now, make a mental note to revisit the issue later when the time is right.

Moving On

Merely stopping things from lowering your score isn't enough if you want to get the highest score possible. In the next chapter, you're going to learn some of the best ways to raise your score to brand new heights!

The Best Ways to Maximize Your Credit Score

The way to gain a good reputation is to endeavor to be what you desire to appear. Socrates

Alright, enough with all the background info!

It's time we got into the main reason you bought the book: how to raise your credit score.

Sure, if you follow the advice you've read so far, odds are you'll raise your score without even trying. But this chapter is packed full of tips to help you take things to the next level.

Ready? Here we go, then!

1. Get a Credit Card

Did you know that a person who doesn't use any credit cards at all is generally seen as a higher risk than someone who has shown that they use credit cards responsibly?

Although surprising at first glance, it kind of makes sense if you think about it.

Part of your credit score is based on the types of credit accounts that you have. It is generally recommended that you try to get experience with different types of credit, and credit cards are one of the easiest forms of credit to obtain. And let's face it, despite the bad rap that credit cards get, they're actually pretty harmless if all you get is a card with a zero monthly fee and pay it off in full each month.

The guy or gal who has never had a credit card is kind of a total unknown — will they pay on time when given credit? Or will they blow it? Potential lenders have no way of knowing, and that makes them nervous.

So don't be an unknown. Show the credit card companies and other lenders that you can be trusted with credit, and that you are able to keep up with your obligations.

2. Use Your Credit Card

See, you can do one better than just having a credit card. If you don't use your credit cards, they won't necessarily help your credit score as much as they should.

The ideal way to use your credit cards is to charge a small amount to them each month, and pay it off in full when you receive your monthly statement. Use your credit cards for everyday purchases that you would have made anyways, such as groceries — this way, you won't be spending any extra money by using them.

Lenders need to know that you are good at making payments on time — and if you have no payments to make because you never actually use your credit card, then lenders won't have a clue. So give them one, and reap the benefits of the good reputation you're building (and higher credit score that goes with it!) the next time you're negotiating a good rate on a mortgage or other loan.

But remember — the key is to only use a small percentage of available credit each month. Try to stick to using 30% or less of available credit.

3. Ask Your Credit Card Company to Raise Your Credit Limit

I know that asking your credit card company to raise your credit limit flies in the face of what many self-respecting credit users would do, right?

Maybe you worry that if you ask for this, they'll think you're about to go on an massively irresponsible shopping spree and max out your card, right?

But the thing is, raising your credit limit while keeping your spending levels the same can actually raise your credit score. This is because part of your credit score is based on the percentage of available credit that you use.

Remember Anna from the previous chapter? She closed a bunch of credit card accounts that she wasn't using, and her credit score dropped, partly because the percentage of available credit that she was using went way up as a result.

So flip that around and use it to your advantage!

Assuming you have a good reputation with your credit card company and tend to pay on time, the odds are good that they'll be happy to accommodate your request for a higher limit. And besides, the worst that can happen is that they say no — aside from wounding your pride, nothing bad will happen.

I used to worry that when I did this, the credit card company would want to know why I wanted the higher limit. But to my surprise, they often don't even ask.

And when they do, my response is usually one of the following:

"I have a large purchase coming up that I'd like to charge to my credit card for the reward points I'll get."

Or,

"I'd just like to have the option of charging larger purchases to my card if I need to — it's cheaper than paying a fee to use my debit card."

And I'm sure you can come up with many more reasons why a larger limit on your card would benefit you.

4. Apply for Another Credit Card

Ok, so in the short term, this can lower your credit score due to the credit check that will be run on you during the application process. But, if your new card has a high enough credit limit, in the long run, your credit score could go up.

You can maximize your chances of a long-term rise in your credit score if you keep your monthly spending the same. This way, the percentage of available credit that you are using will decrease — and that is the secret sauce to raising your score via this method.

This strategy is best if:

- You can afford to take a small hit to your credit score in the

short-term (i.e., your score will decrease at first, due to the credit check that will be run on you).
- You will not increase your spending just because you have access to more credit.

Caution

If you implement this strategy, I recommend that you go slow — add one new account at a time, and monitor the effects that it has on your credit score.

Assuming all goes according to plan and your score rises in a few months, feel free to apply for another credit card. Wait and see what the effect is on your credit score this time (I recommend you wait a good six months to be sure of the effects), and if it rises, feel free to add another credit card to your collection.

Many experts recommend limiting your total number of credit cards to no more than three to five. But the thing is, there is no 100% hard and fast rule about this — everyone's credit file is different, and the algorithms that the credit bureaus use to calculate your score are very complex, thus making it hard to predict with certainty how many cards are too many for any one individual.

By adding one card at a time, and waiting several months in between adding a new account, you ensure that you minimize any risks by monitoring the results of any changes you make, and being able to backtrack if needed.

I do not recommend that you add new accounts if you are planning on applying for important credit in the near future, such as a mortgage.

The Key To Success With This Strategy

Here are the keys to maximizing your odds of success with this strategy:

- Charge a small amount to the new credit card, and pay it off in full each month.
- Ensure that your total spending across all credit accounts does not increase. (For example, if, before obtaining the new card, you charged $1000 in total per month to all of your credit cards combined, continue to charge no more than $1000 per month in total to all of your credit cards combined.)
- Pay off the balance on all of your credit cards in full, and on time, when you get your monthly statements.

5. Pay Off Your Credit Cards In Full Each Month

Being close to maxing out your credit cards is worse than using a small amount of your available credit. You see, people who are close to maxing out their credit cards are associated with a higher risk of defaulting or not being able to make future payments.

On the other hand, if you not only limit yourself to using a small amount of your available credit each month, and you pay off your credit cards in full, you'll be lumped in with the lower risk people and end up with a higher credit score than you would if you left that balance to grow with time.

The thing is, if you don't pay off your credit cards in full each month, odds are, the percentage of available credit that you are using will creep up every month.

And as you can imagine, that percentage creep is likely to lower your credit score.

For example, Matt charges $500 each month to his credit card. He only makes the minimum payments, and within less than a year he ends up owing a few thousand dollars.

This is his only credit card, and the limit is $5000. Within 10 months, he's easily maxed out his card, and that leads to a fall in his credit score.

So don't be like Matt. Pay off your credit card in full each month and enjoy the higher credit score that should result.

6. Keep Credit Balances to Less Than 30% of the Maximum Available Credit

Experts recommend keeping your credit balances to less than 30% of your maximum limit. Your credit score can take a moderate hit if the balance goes over 50%, and major hit if the balance goes over 75%.

7. Experience With Both Revolving and Installment Accounts Is Good

Part of your credit score is based on the types of credit accounts that you have experience with. By having experience with multiple kinds of credit, you can raise your score more than you would if you lacked variety on your credit report.

You can start things off by getting some experience with credit cards, a type of revolving account.

Lines of Credit

A line of credit from your local bank is another kind of revolving account. I love lines of credit for the simple fact that having one on my checking account means I never have to worry about overdrawing my account with day-to-day purchases. And if its responsible use adds some variety to my credit report, all the better.

As long as you have the willpower not to max out your line of credit just because it's there, you ought to consider getting one if you haven't already.

Secured Installment Loans

Secured installment accounts include things like a car loan — whatever you are borrowing the money for is used as collateral for the loan (i.e., if you default on your loan, the lender gets the item you borrowed the money for in the first place). In addition to that, you'll have a fixed amount that you need to pay off each and every month, and the balance owing on the loan will decrease in time, until it reaches zero.

Secured installment loans can be a great way to increase your credit score because showing your ability to make a fixed monthly payment is an indicator of your reliability and financial stability.

This is very different from a credit card, where a person can vary the amount of their payments each month, depending on their cash flow.

Due to the interest charges you'll incur, I don't recommend that most people go out and get an installment loan just for the sake of helping their credit score. But, if you ever do require such a loan, it's nice to know that it might help your credit score in the long run. Another thing to remember is that part of your credit score is based on the percentage of available credit that you use — so the benefit of an installment loan will go up as you pay down the loan, thus making your percentage of available credit being used decrease.

Warning: Don't Be Trapped By an Upside Down Loan!

An upside down loan is when the amount you owe is more than you can get by selling the item that the loan was taken out to purchase.

For example, Michael owns a house worth $300,000 and accidentally ended up with an upside down loan.

He owes $250,000 on his mortgage, plus he got a home-equity loan to buy a boat for $30,000. And in addition to that, he has a line of credit against his home which he maxed out to buy a motorhome for $80,000.

If for any reason he runs into financial trouble and misses too many payments on his home equity loan for his boat, he could be forced into selling his home to repay the loan.

But you see the trouble he's in if that happens, right?

His home is only worth $300,000 in the current market — yet if he sells his home for that, he'll owe the bank $350,000 ($250,000 + $30,000 + $80.000). Sure, he could sell the boat and motorhome, but they've fallen in value since he bought them so he won't be able to come up with all of the money he owes that way.

Anna also ran into trouble with an upside down loan. She bought her car brand new for $35,000 and used a car loan to finance 100% of the cost over five years. But a year later, she lost her job and could no longer afford the car payments. She tries to sell her car, but you know how it is with new cars, right? A year later, it's worth less than the amount she still owes on her car loan (she can only get $28,000 for it!). So even if she sells, she'll have to figure out some way to come up with the extra money that will still be owed.

How To Avoid Upside Down Loans

You can dramatically reduce your odds of becoming victimized by an upside down loan.

If you buy a home, try to put a large downpayment on it. That way, even if home values fall and you have to sell your home for some reason, odds are better that the sales proceeds will provide enough money to pay off the mortgage balance.

The same goes for buying a car.

Financing anything by 100% is risky — putting a large downpayment on it will dramatically reduce your odds of finding yourself in the upside down loan trap.

8. Minimize "Hard Inquiries" on Your Credit Report

Minimize the number of "hard inquiries" on your credit report. Hard inquiries occur when a lender is checking your credit report to finalize your application for credit with them — this will lower your score temporarily.

For example, when you apply for a new credit card, the credit card company will often check your credit score before deciding whether or not to grant you a card.

When renting a car, if you plan on paying via debit card, many rental companies will run a credit report on you to see if you're likely to pay your debts. Whereas if you pay via credit card, they generally don't bother since they know they can put a hold on your card for the amount of the rental, insurance, gas, etc.

Cool fact #1: If you'll be applying for several credit cards in the near future, you might want to consider applying for them all in the same day. Often, hard credit inquiries made in a short period of time will only count as a single hard inquiry on your credit report, so will lower it less than spreading out those same inquiries over several weeks.

Cool fact #2: If you're shopping around for a good rate on a mortgage, the lender may check your credit before telling you what rate they're willing to offer you. These types of inquiries are considered a "soft" inquiry, and they do not affect your credit score in the slightest. Only once you decide which bank to take out a mortgage with will they do a "hard" credit inquiry to confirm everything.

9. Always Make Your Payments on Time

You're probably rolling your eyes at this one — because really, *everyone* knows this right? But this one is so important (albeit obvious), that I felt the list wouldn't be complete without including it — payment history makes up 35% of your FICO score, after all!

The longer you are making payments on time for a loan, the higher your score can go. Not only does the fact that your balance is decreasing help, but the longer your record of on-time payments, the more trustworthy you become in the eyes of the credit bureaus.

Credit Scores Can Be Forgiving

But before we move on, I just wanted to say that if by some chance you've messed up in the past and made some late payments, please don't throw in the towel!

As long as you start making your payments on time today, and keep it that way, your score will rise over time. In fact, the longer you keep your accounts paid up to date, the more your score should rise. FICO gives more weight to current credit habits than old ones. Generally speaking, the previous 24 months of payments are the most important — so not only will your current good habits add to the positive factors in your score, they will also dilute the impact of any previous mistakes.

10. Sooner Is Better Than Later for Late Payments

If you must make a late payment, the sooner you do it, the better —

late payments are measured in either 30, 60, or 90 day increments, and the longer you wait to pay it, the worse of an impact it has on your credit score.

11. Some Late Payments Are Worse Than Others

If there's no way to avoid it and you absolutely must pay something late this month, then keep your credit score as high as possible by being strategic about which bill you choose to pay late.

Often, mortgage payments less than 15 days late are not reported to the credit bureaus, nor are late payments for utility bills (unless they tell you they'll be sending your account to a collection agency).

But keep in mind that if you do end up being late enough on your mortgage payments to be considered in default, it's considered a very serious delinquency on your credit report.

If you feel forced into making a decision like this, confirm the policies of whatever creditor whose bill you're thinking of paying late before making a final decision. I know you might feel embarrassed to make a call like that, but trust me, you're not the first, nor will you be the last person to be in this predicament. And anyone worth their salt will see you as more responsible for being honest and facing this situation head on, compared to being frozen in fear and unwilling to take the necessary steps. So go ahead and make the call — it'll be worth it to save your credit score!

Once you're on the phone, explain when you'll be able to pay them, and that you want to know if paying "x" number of days late will be reported to the credit bureaus. Worst case, if they say even one day late is enough to be reported to the credit bureaus, move on to your next creditor and ask about their policy instead.

12. Be Predictable

Say you've gone through a bad spell with your finances and have missed a few payments in a row. Some experts say doing that is better than being unpredictable, missing payments randomly and intermittently. Some say that if you make a several late payments in a row, it is sometimes counted as a single late payment for the purposes of calculating your credit score.

It makes sense if you think about it — missing payments two months in a row might mean you lost your job, or had some other temporary issue that affected your ability to manage your money — that is, it might not be *you* causing the problem, but just a bad situation.

But say you miss a payment in January, May, and September — this might indicate that you have ongoing cash management issues, so it could be frowned upon more by the credit reporting agencies.

I'm not suggesting that you test this out; the rules could change any time, after all. But, I figured it couldn't hurt to mention this since it might console you somewhat if you've been in this situation.

And you also should know that even if each missed payment doesn't show up in the credit score itself, it is still likely to show up on your credit report. This is because most accounts show whether or not each payment in the previous two years was paid on time or not.

So the score itself might take only a single hit if you miss several payments in a row, but your credit report can still show all the details of how many payments were missed, and when.

Makes sense? Ok, onwards then…

13. Reduce Your Total Debt

We've discussed credit cards at length, but there's more to your debt than just credit cards, right?

There's student loans, car loans, mortgages… the list goes on!

You know how the lower the percentage of available credit you use, the higher your score can rise, right? Well, that applies to your student loans, car loan, and mortgage too! The credit score gods will reward you with a higher score for showing that you are willing and able to pay off debt.

So if the freedom you'll feel when you pay off those debts isn't enough motivation, think of the rise in credit score that can be yours!

Vantage recommends that your total debt should remain at no more than 30% of available credit on each account. TransUnion suggests sticking with 35% or less. I say be conservative and aim for 30% or less — that ought to make everyone happy!

Debt Reduction Strategy

When reducing your debts with the primary purpose of increasing your credit score, your main priority should be to get all account balances to a level that is smiled upon by the credit bureaus.

You now know that the "safe zone" is to have no balances exceed 30% of your credit limit. Anything above 50% of your credit limit is worse.

So, start by paying down any credit cards with balances that exceed 50%. Once you have them down to say, 45%, move on to the next card. Once all cards have balances that are less than 45%, start working on getting their balances down to 30% or less of the credit limit. After that, pay them off one by one.

If, on the other hand, you are paying down your credit cards solely to reduce debt, but you don't need to worry about the immediate impact on your credit score, you should generally pay down the cards with the highest interest rates first to save money on interest charges.

14. Minimize Accounts With Balances

A higher number of accounts with balances can mean a higher risk of over-extension — so to maximize your credit score, keep the number of credit accounts that carry a balance to a minimum.

Of course, as with everything in the world of credit scores, what number of accounts with balances is too high will vary from person to person.

Her are some factors that you should keep in mind:

i) The thinner your credit file, the more of an impact accounts with balances are likely to have.

ii) The larger the percentage of available credit you are using, the more of an impact it will have on your credit score. Say you have three credit cards, each with a credit limit of $5000. Carrying a balance of $100 on each of them won't affect your credit score as much as carrying a balance of $4000 on each of your three credit cards will.

15. Paying Off Debt Is Better Than Moving It Around

Paying off debt (for example, credit card debt) is better than transferring it to another loan product or credit card. This is because paying it off keeps the percentage of available credit being used lower, which helps to raise your score.

Action Steps:

1. Go through each of the factors discussed in this list, and make a list of which ones make sense to implement right now.

2. Make another list of factors that you want to implement at a later date, when the time is right.

Moving On

After reading through this book, almost everyone will have enough information to climb out of the low credit score hole and into the realm of good credit.

But what if your situation is particularly dire? What if this is a good start, but it won't get you all the way to the finish line?

Then the next chapter is for you.

How to Find a Reputable Credit Counselor (That Won't Hurt Your Credit Score)

Learning is not attained by chance, it must be sought for with ardor and diligence. Abigail Adams

If you're in really dire straights, although this book will help to put you on the right track to raising your credit score, it might not be enough. This is where consulting with a reputable credit counselor comes in.

Credit counselors can be an enormous help if you're in the unfortunate situation of having no way to make all of the payments that you owe on time. If your only other alternative is bankruptcy, they can help you avoid that by helping you to come up with a plan to manage and pay down your debts responsibly. They can also help you with contacting creditors to figure out a mutually agreeable solution, among other things. Basically, they're there to help you dig yourself out of this hole, to help you weather this storm.

The mere act of getting credit counseling will not hurt your FICO score. It's what you do as a result of that counseling that can hurt it. So choose your credit counselor wisely, and avoid damaging your credit by implementing wrong-headed advice.

The trouble is, there are too many greedy scammers out there who make a living by preying on desperate people. I don't want you to end up as one of their victims, so here is how you sidestep them and find a credit counselor that you can trust.

One more thing…

Although the use of a credit counselor will not hurt your FICO score, if the use of a credit counselor shows up on your credit report, future lenders may frown upon it, worrying that if you needed to resort to using a credit counselor, you aren't able to manage your debts as agreed upon.

So only pursue this route if it's the lesser evil — for example, if your alternative is bankruptcy, and credit counseling can help you avoid that, credit counseling would likely be the lesser evil.

Government Recommended or Sanctioned Credit Counseling Agencies

Anyone can make a slick website that looks professional to trick you into thinking you can trust in their expertise. The good news is, you can easily weed out the scammers by only considering those agencies that are recommended in some way by the government. Here are a few that you should take a look at.

1. Hope Now

Hope Now is an organization that was formed via an alliance between credit counselors, mortgage companies, and other participants in the mortgage market. This alliance was encouraged by the US government to help create solutions that would solve mortgage problems.

They help troubled homeowners find solutions that will allow them to stay in their homes.

If you've made some late payments on your mortgage, or are at risk of missing any, take a look at what Hope Now can offer you. Here is their website: www.hopenow.com.

2. The National Council of State Housing Agencies

These guys can be a great help in providing you with support for any housing finance questions or concerns. You can search by state to find the agency nearest you. Check out what they can offer here: www.ncsha.org/housing-help.

3. HUD-approved Counseling Services

HUD-approved counseling services can provide you with advice on defaults, foreclosures, and general credit issues, among other things.

http://www.hud.gov/offices/hsg/sfh/hcc/hcs.cfm

4. The Department of Justice

The Department of Justice also has some great tips for finding reputable sources of credit counseling.

http://www.justice.gov/ust/eo/bapcpa/ccde/index.htm

Credit Counselors Vetted by Professional or Consumer Organizations

Next, take a look at credit counselors that have been vetted by professional or consumer organizations.

1. The National Foundation for Credit Counseling

The National Foundation for Credit Counseling is the oldest nonprofit financial counseling organization in the United States, with a focus on providing free or affordably priced services. They can be of help with a diverse range of credit problems, including:

- Credit/debt counseling
- Bankruptcy counseling
- Housing counseling
- Reverse mortgage counseling
- Student loan debt counseling
- Debt management plans
- Credit report reviews
- Financial education

For more details, check out their website at www.nfcc.org

2. The Financial Counseling Association of America

Formerly known as the Association of Independent Consumer Credit Counseling Agencies, the Financial Counseling Association of America is the largest national association representing non-profit credit counseling companies.

They can be of help with:

- Bankruptcy counseling
- Credit counseling
- Credit report reviews
- Debt management plans
- Financial education

- Housing counseling
- Reverse mortgage counseling
- Student loans counseling

For more information, visit their website at www.fcaa.org

Beware of Debt Settlement Plans

Beware of Debt Settlement Plans where you pay a lump sum to a company that purports to "help" you by holding onto your money, without making any payments to your creditors, until they agree out of desperation to stop hounding you.

The companies that offer this service may say you'll get off easier with a smaller payment and save money in the long run, but even if they pull this off, essentially holding your money hostage instead of making payments can trash your credit score.

You're better off trying to work with your creditors to come up with a payment plan that you can maintain, and that results in them getting the money they are owed. Everyone is happy that way, and you'll minimize or prevent any damage to your credit score.

Beware of Unscrupulous Credit Repair Companies

These guys sound great — who wouldn't want someone to "repair" their damaged credit, right?

The problem with many of these companies is that they try to fix your credit by challenging all of the negative things on it — anything that is not verifiable in the legal timeframe will be removed in as little as 30 days.

Perfect, right?

Not really.

Because what happens is that the credit bureaus will continue to try and verify the challenged information — and if it turns out that the info they removed was, in fact, accurate, it'll be put right back on your credit report just like before.

And worse, if you successfully applied for credit based on a credit report with missing information (due to those challenges filed on your behalf by the Credit Repair Company), you could be charged with fraud. Because you can be held legally responsible for any action you take, even if it's on the advice of a credit repair company.

Additionally, credit repair companies can be expensive.

And finally, you're risking identity theft by sharing your credit history with a stranger. The credit repair industry is not well regulated, so the credentials of whoever you end up dealing with may not be reputable.

As you can see, dealing with a credit repair company is a potential disaster in the making, and best avoided!

The thing these guys don't want you to know is that the best way to permanently repair your credit is to do it yourself or with the help of a *reputable* credit counselor from a source such as the ones listed earlier in this chapter.

The Pitfalls of Starting Over With a Brand New EIN Number

Another illegal ploy sometimes suggested by disreputable credit counseling and repair companies without a conscience is that you start over with a brand new EIN number for all credit applications going forward.

The idea is, you stop using your old social security number, and use a brand spanking new EIN number instead, which won't have all of your previous bad credit history on it.

But this could get you into hot water with the law, so aside from being dishonest, it isn't worth the potential legal hassles that will likely ensue from it.

Remember, there are far better, legal ways to improve your credit score, even if your life has fallen apart and you're starting out with a disastrously low credit score.

Do These Things First Before You Hire a Credit Counselor

There are a few things you should always do before hiring a credit counselor.

First, contact your state Attorney General's Office and local Better Business Bureau to find out more about this particular credit counselor's reputation. Also, ask if there are any complaints against them, and whether or not they were resolved.

Secondly, find out what kind of fees you'll be expected to pay for their services.

Thirdly, find out how and when your creditors will be paid — get this information in writing. You need to know this information so that you can follow up and ensure that they do what they say they will do.

Lastly, if credit counseling is a last ditch effort to avoid bankruptcy, it might also be worthwhile to consult with a lawyer who specializes in bankruptcy proceedings, to discuss other legal options. They can also be a great sounding board for any suggestions that the credit counseling agency has made to you.

Remember This

Even if, worst case scenario, you have made a ton of mistakes and are totally humiliated right now due to poor credit, stay strong. You can bounce back from this.

Sure, you might not bounce back as fast as you like, but this doesn't have to be a life sentence.

So whatever your situation might be, assess the situation, come up with a plan or two, choose the best course of action, and then take action.

And don't forget to implement the strategies in this book — your credit score *will* rise eventually. And yes, it can even become a great credit score, given enough time.

Remember, even a bankruptcy will only stay on your credit report for 10 years at worst. Sure, that's a major bummer. But if you do all the right things while that 10 year clock is ticking, you can come out of it with a good credit score.

And isn't that worth fighting for?

Because once you have that good credit score, all you have to do is maintain it, and you'll be able to enjoy it for the rest of your life.

So whatever you do, do not give up, ok?

There's One More Thing That You MUST Do

To finish up, I'd like to say that while the tips in this book will go a long way to helping you to raise your credit score, there is one more thing that you absolutely MUST do, if you're not doing it already.

Because the thing is, many people with credit problems, if they dig into it deep enough, find that most of their credit problems started because they were living paycheck-to-paycheck.

Living paycheck-to-paycheck increases the odds that any financial hiccups will cause you to miss payments on your debt, or max out your credit lines, both of which can trash your credit score over time.

If you're serious about raising your credit score, and keeping it high over the long term, then you've got to come up with a plan that will allow you to master your money once and for all, and stop living paycheck-to-paycheck.

If you're stuck in that trap, the best-selling first book in the *Smart Money Blueprint* series, *How to Stop Living Paycheck to Paycheck*, can help you get out of it.

It's been read by thousands of people, has been featured on live radio in New York City, and can change your financial life forever.

Smart Money Blueprint: How to Stop Living Paycheck to Paycheck will teach you time-tested money management techniques that will aid in protecting your credit score by helping to ensure that you never run out of money to pay your debts. And best of all, these simple techniques take only 15 minutes a week to maintain.

What people are saying about *Smart Money Blueprint: How to Stop Living Paycheck to Paycheck*:

"Avery Breyer just could be a godsend to most of us who are living paycheck to paycheck while the rich get richer and the poor get poorer. Finally someone has come up with some practical, easy, quick, and workable suggestions to get out of debt and stay there." Grady Harp (Hall of Fame, Amazon Top 100 Reviewer, Vine Voice)

"This is the rarest of all rarities — a really good ebook on personal finance." Amazon Top 1000 Reviewer

"Avery Breyer's self-help guide to consumer finances... is filled with great ideas for getting out of a financial rut. I found her reasons for setting up a budget to be compelling and was impressed by the Money Tracker program she includes with the book... It's highly recommended." Rated 5-stars by Jack Magnus (Readers' Favorite)

"I needed this book 25 years ago!" David Woody (Amazon Reader)

So **check it out** — and if you like what you see, give it a read.

http://www.amazon.com/dp/B00Y2OR2H4/

Here is a sample of the book:

Introduction for *Smart Money Blueprint: How To Stop Living Paycheck to Paycheck*

Do you want to learn proven techniques that will help you to stop living paycheck to paycheck and stop stressing out about money?

Do you want to be able to relax, knowing that all of your needs, today and in the future, can be paid for with ease?

Look, we've all gone through tough times with money, but the good news is that it doesn't have to be that way.

Maybe credit card debt is the only way you are able to keep afloat right now, although you know that's not a long-term solution. Maybe you feel ashamed that you're not doing a better job of managing your money — you feel frustrated that you can't get ahead. And maybe you've tried budgeting, but it just didn't work for you.

This book is going to show you solutions that actually work.

This book will provide you with both the tools and the knowledge that you need to finally get ahead.

You'll learn a step-by-step system that is easy to implement, and takes only one hour a month to maintain (15 minutes once per week). I promise you that if you read this book and follow the advice in here, you'll be set on a path to a world where you control your money, you have a plan that will ensure you don't run out of money, and you are no longer a slave to your bills.

Stand up to your obstacles and do something about them. You will find that they haven't half the strength you think they have.
Norman Vincent Peale

Why I Wrote This Book

It kills me to see people in financial trouble, when they could have easily avoided it if only they'd had the tools and the knowledge to prevent it.

I was lucky to be raised in a family that believed in the power of saving and budgeting, and taught me all of their skills, tips, and tricks. And now I want to share those lucky teachings with you — because they are life-changing, and they work. They work when you are starting out with no money, no assets, zip, zero, zilch. And they work later, when you pull yourself out of that situation to a life of more abundance.

This book is based on those lessons, and my success in implementing those strategies in my own life. I've been successfully using these strategies for over 20 years now, and I can tell you, they work.

My hope is that if you're in a world of financial hurt right now, the strategies I share in this book will help you get out of it, and start living the life you want. Just remember that it will take time, practice, and hard work — but all of it will be well worth it in the end!

He who would learn to fly one day must first learn to stand and walk and run and climb and dance; one cannot fly into flying. Friedrich Nietzsche

Who Should Read This Book

This book is for you if :

- You are living paycheck to paycheck and struggling to pay your bills (but you know that so, onwards…).
- You'd like to use a budgeting system that's easy to use and actually works.
- You want to be in control of your money, rather than have your money control you.
- You feel like your money isn't stretching as far as it should.
- You have one hour per month (15 minutes per week) to put towards maintaining the budgeting system that you'll learn in this book.
- You're having trouble reaching your financial goals.

This Book is NOT For You If

This book is definitely not for you if you want to be taught all about how to invest your money. That is a totally separate topic, and deserves a book of its own!

My view is that before you can even think about investing your money, you need to stop living paycheck to paycheck — and this book will help you do that. Once you've mastered the art of managing your money via a budget that runs like a well-oiled machine, then, and only then, should you start to learn about investing your money. I'll recommend some reading for that at the end of this book!

This book is not for you if you want a magic elixir that will fix everything for you overnight.

This book is not for you if you want advice from someone who is currently broke and living paycheck to paycheck. Wouldn't you rather take your budgeting advice from someone who has figured out how to make their money work for them, and can teach you exactly how they did it so you can do the same? I use these money management strategies every day and they work very well. Let me show you how to do it!

Last, but not least, remember this: For the strategies in this book to be maximally effective, you need to be committed to learning the techniques that this book will teach you, and you need to be willing to stick with it over the long haul.

Never Give Up

Now, I know that you might be one of those people who are in a really tough situation that it seems only a fairy godmother could fix. But if you look deep inside yourself, can you say with 100% certainty that you are doing absolutely everything (and I mean everything!) within your power to maximize the benefits that whatever money you have can provide you with? Is there a chance that your frustration with your financial situation might have caused you to give up on yourself? Is it possible that your financial situation has caused you to lose hope that it can ever get better and you've stopped trying to improve it?

If any of that sounds like you, then I ask you to give yourself another chance at a life that's free from stressing about money.

You're stronger and more capable than you think.

You deserve another chance. Give it to yourself. Never give up.

The strategies that you'll learn in this book can go a long way towards ensuring you get to live a life that's free from most of the stresses about money.

What You Will Learn in This Book

By reading this book, you're going to learn the easy way to put together a budget that will:

- help you pay down bad debt, and avoid getting more
- help you reach your financial goals with greater ease
- provide for your daily monetary needs, both now, and in the future
- lower or eliminate your worries about money
- take an hour per month or less to keep tabs on
- actually work

You will also learn:

- the 6 most important things you can do to take control of your money
- the 5 biggest benefits to having a budget
- the common misconceptions about budgets
- 10 tips on how to get the right mindset for success
- 11 budget traps, and how to avoid them
- the easiest ways to have more money without earning more
- how to trim your expenses with (almost) no effort
- how to use our free tool, the Money Tracker, to make your own custom system for taking control of your money
- tips that will help you eliminate your debts

My Promise to You

I promise you that if you read this book, and stick with the strategies you'll learn from it, you will dramatically increase your odds of having a more secure financial future and a lot less stress about money in your life.

Don't be the kind of person who procrastinates and makes a bad situation worse.

Be the kind of person who isn't afraid to to tackle a problem head on.

Be the kind of person whom others admire for their tenacity and determination to overcome any roadblocks in their path, and push through to success.

Be the kind of person who takes action now.

The strategies you will learn in this book can create positive, long-lasting results. All you need to do right now to reap those rewards is keep reading.

You can stop living paycheck to paycheck and start to take control of your money right now, today. After that, sit back and enjoy the new life you are creating for yourself, a life where you feel secure and more confident in your ability to manage your money. It's your time.

Buy the book today, and change your life forever!

http://www.amazon.com/dp/B00Y2OR2H4/

Did You Enjoy This Book?

I want to thank you for purchasing and reading this book. I really hope you got a lot out of it!

Can I ask you for a quick favour though?

If you enjoyed this book, I would really appreciate it if you could leave me a review on Amazon.

I love getting feedback from my readers, and reviews on Amazon really do make a difference. I read all of my reviews and would really love to hear your thoughts.

Thanks so much!

Avery Breyer

P.S. You can go here (http://www.amazon.com/dp/B00Y2OR2H4/) to go directly to the book on Amazon and leave your review.

Thank-You For Reading My Book!

Just to say thanks for buying my book, I'd like to give you **a free audiobook version of** *Smart Money Blueprint: How to Raise Your Credit Score.*

I think you'll find it handy to have for those times when you need your hands free, but are in the mood to "read" this book.

Get it here!

http://averybreyer.com/how-to-raise-your-credit-score-opt-in/

15005449R00057

Printed in Great Britain
by Amazon.co.uk, Ltd.,
Marston Gate.